D0349956

CITIZEN CANINE
DOGS IN THE MOVIES
WENDY MITCHELL

Laurence King Publishing

Published by
Laurence King Publishing
361–373 City Road
London EC1V 1LR
United Kingdom
T +44 20 7841 6900
enquiries@laurenceking.com
www.laurenceking.com

A catalogue record for this book
is available from the British Library.

ISBN: 978 1 78627 574 5

Design: Katerina Kerouli
and Florian Michelet

Printed in China

Laurence King Publishing is committed to
ethical and sustainable production.
We are proud participants in The Book
Chain Project ®
bookchainproject.com

Contents

Scraps
A Dog's Life
8

Lobo
*The Clash of
the Wolves*
10

Strongheart
*The Return
of Boston Blackie*
12

Petey
Dogs Is Dogs
14

George
Bringing Up Baby
16

Toto
The Wizard of Oz
18

Lassie
Lassie Come Home
20

Flike
Umberto D
22

Yeller
Old Yeller
24

Bobby
*Greyfriars Bobby:
The True Story
of a Dog*
26

Red
Big Red
28

Sounder
Sounder
30

Digby
*Digby: The Biggest
Dog in the World*
32

**Old Dan &
Little Ann**
*Where the Red
Fern Grows*
34

Benji
Benji
36

Sandy
Annie
38

White dog
White Dog
40

Cujo
Cujo
42

Matisse
*Down and Out in
Beverly Hills*
44

Hooch
Turner & Hooch
46

Jerry Lee
K-9
48

White Fang
White Fang
50

Beethoven
Beethoven
52

Chance
*Homeward Bound:
The Incredible Journey*
54

Yellow
*Far From Home:
The Adventures
of Yellow Dog*
56

Fly
Babe
58

The puppies
101 Dalmations
60

Buddy
Air Bud
62

Zeus
Zeus and Roxanne
64

Verdell
As Good As It Gets
66

Puffy
*There's Something
About Mary*
68

Patrasche
A Dog of Flanders
70

**Winky, Miss
Agnes, Beatrice
& Hubert**
Best in Show
72

Mr Beefy
Little Nicky
74

Skip
My Dog Skip
76

Lou
Cats & Dogs
78

Frank
Men In Black II
80

Bruiser
*Legally Blonde 2: Red,
White & Blonde*
82

Bombón
Bombón El Perro
84

Winn-Dixie
*Because of
Winn-Dixie*
86

Maya
Eight Below
88

Shaggy
The Shaggy Dog
90

Sam
I Am Legend
92

Papi
Beverly Hills Chihuahua
94

Lucy
Wendy & Lucy
96

Marley
Marley & Me
98

Hachi
Hachi: A Dog's Tale
100

Romeo
Hotel For Dogs
102

Arthur
Beginners
104

Marmaduke
Marmaduke
106

The Dog
The Artist
108

Red Dog
Red Dog
110

Banjo
Sightseers
112

Bonny
Seven Psychopaths
114

Hagen
White God
116

Rocco
The Drop
118

Max
Max
120

Wiener-Dog
Wiener-Dog
122

Bailey
A Dog's Purpose
124

Patrick
Patrick
126

Introduction

I love films. And I adore dogs. So when the two come together, I'm in heaven (and usually floods of tears). Can you blame me? Even the coldest of hearts can be melted by a charming cinematic canine: Alfred Hitchcock, the curtain-slashing genius behind *Psycho*, revealed he was a fan of Benji, that sweet stray mutt.

Dogs can teach us life lessons about loyalty, unconditional love and bonds that can last after death. They can also do silly tricks, if that's what you prefer.

There's a purity, an innocence, to a dog on screen. With particularly skilled canine actors, you can pick up their emotions. Other times they can be more like a blank slate on which we can powerfully project our own emotions.

This book celebrates a diverse range of canine acting over the last one hundred years, from naturalistic performances like Cosmo's look of pure love for Ewan McGregor in *Beginners*; to complicated action manoeuvres like Pal's famous river scene in *Lassie Come Home*.

Dogs heighten a movie's emotional impact, whether in happy films (Chaplin's *A Dog's Life*), sad films (*Old Yeller,* sniff sniff), funny films (Uggie in *The Artist*) or scary films (Cujo, the slobbering Saint Bernard of our nightmares).

As Lassie trainer Rudd Weatherwax wrote, referring to the power of dog stars: 'A dog can say more with his eyes than can a human with a dozen pages written by the cleverest writers.'

This book celebrates these talented pooches, the caring and dedicated trainers who bring out the best in them, and the actors and directors who find the best way to work with their canine co-stars on set.

We all know W.C. Fields' famous advice, 'Never work with children or animals.' They never tell you the next line: 'They'll upstage you every time.'

Here's a celebration of the best scene stealers.

Wendy Mitchell

Scraps
A Dog's Life, 1918

Breed: Mixed Breed

Any animal that can match Charlie Chaplin for physical comedy is a true star. Scraps, the 'thoroughbred mongrel', displays timing as impeccable as Chaplin's himself – jumping up to steal a string of sausages, swirling at the centre of a chaotic dog fight, letting himself be stuffed down Chaplin's trousers, offering himself as a pillow, hitting the dancefloor with Chaplin and his love Edna, or fetching a money-stuffed wallet. All this before CGI was invented.

The title alludes more to Chaplin's character than the canine; there are poignant parallels between the street dog and down-on-his-luck street dweller, the Tramp. It's no wonder they become inseparable companions, stealing food and evading the cops together.

There are poignant parallels between the street dog and down-on-his-luck street dweller, the Tramp.

Before finding a male rescue dog named Mut, Chaplin had screen-tested a dachshund, a Pomeranian, a poodle, a Boston bull terrier and an English bulldog. He said, 'what I really wanted is a mongrel dog. These studio beasts are too well kept.'

It was, sadly, Mut's only film role: after shooting *A Dog's Life*, Chaplin left on a tour selling war bonds; Mut was so sad that he refused to eat, dying three weeks later of a supposed 'broken heart'.

 Growth spurt: Mut started the film as a puppy and grew quickly during the making of it, so the team had to use oversized props and special camera angles for shooting the end of the film.

 Hands on: The Tramp is seen without his trademark cane because Chaplin needed his hand free to hold onto Scraps' leash.

Lobo
The Clash of the Wolves, 1925

Breed: German Shepherd

Rin Tin Tin is a Hollywood legend for good reason – he was an exceptional performer with an exceptional biography.

US army man Lee Duncan was serving in France at the end of World War I, when he found a litter of German shepherd puppies in a bombed-out kennel. Duncan brought one of those puppies, who he named Rin Tin Tin, back to California and noticed how trainable the dog was.

Rin Tin Tin's first major role came with 1923's *Where the North Begins*, which became a hit that saved a struggling Warner Bros. Soon, Rin Tin Tin was earning

Rin Tin Tin received 50,000 fan letters a month.

more than human superstars and receiving 50,000 fan letters a month.

The Clash of the Wolves is a great showcase for his talents – it's one of only six of Rin Tin Tin's 26 silent films that survives today. The story revolves around Lobo, a half-breed wolf who leads a pack until a prospector needs his help. The action is amazing: watch him dashing unbelievably quickly across the desert, leaping down a hill, then climbing a tree. Yes, climbing a tree! He can also look soulful and forlorn.

Susan Orlean, who authored a fascinating biography of Rinty, said, 'No matter how skeptical you could be about if a dog could convey emotion, he really does.'

 Oscar snub: Rin Tin Tin was so popular in Hollywood that he is said to have received the most votes for the Best Actor Oscar in 1929. However, the Academy decided the award had to go to a human.

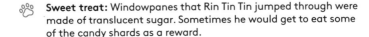 **Sweet treat:** Windowpanes that Rin Tin Tin jumped through were made of translucent sugar. Sometimes he would get to eat some of the candy shards as a reward.

Strongheart

The Return of Boston Blackie, 1927

Breed: German Shepherd

Strongheart made six feature films between 1921 and 1927. He became a multi-millionaire and Hollywood's highest-grossing star (including humans!). His final starring role is also his only

Strongheart gives a performance that's both emotional and athletic.

surviving film. *The Return of Boston Blackie* is about a gangster getting out of prison, reuniting with his loyal dog, and getting drawn into a necklace theft.

Even though the imposing 125-pound Strongheart isn't the star of the film in terms of screen time (he still got top billing), he gives a performance that's both emotional and athletic. He bolts down a road to rescue his master, rips the clothes off a bad guy, sails around a fairground ride, swims in the ocean, steals a string of sausages, jumps through a window to escape a fire, and admires himself in a funhouse mirror.

Strongheart was born Etzel von Oeringen in Poland and then worked in the Berlin police force and the German Red Cross before being sent to a kennel in America. Filmmakers Larry Trimble and Jane Murfin discovered him there. They renamed him, retrained him and launched his film career with 1921 hit *The Silent Call*.

Stronheart is still remembered as the first famous acting canine who was beloved around the globe.

 Soft touch: Strongheart was a strong dog but knew how to be gentle. Trimble said, 'His human counterparts on screen were pleased with Strongheart, for even though he tore their clothes to shreds, he never left a mark of fang or nail on any actor.'

 Silent star: It's a shame Strongheart's bark won't be heard for posterity, as all of his films were made in the silent era.

Petey
Dogs Is Dogs, 1931

Breed: American Pit Bull Terrier

Petey the dog was an integral member of Hal Roach's Rascals, also known as Our Gang and later the Little Rascals, and he gets a large role in one of their best short films of the 1930s, *Dogs Is Dogs*.

Wheezer and Dorothy are living with their mean stepmother, who won't even let Wheezer's beloved dog Petey in the house. She slurs that he's 'nothing but an alley dog', although she pampers her own son Spud and his pedigreed pooch Nero.

Petey's a precise actor, with great timing on actions like licking his chops, looking in through a window, nuzzling Wheezer's feet, having a pillow fight, or modelling a fancy harness.

The Our Gang shorts started in 1922 starring Pal the dog (*not* the Pal of Lassie fame). When Pal died in 1930, his son Pete became Petey from the age of six months, going on to appear in dozens of Our Gang classics.

Owner Harry Lucenay trained Petey to deliver flawless moves to verbal commands and then re-taught him all the tricks to hand commands during the transition from silent films to talkies.

The kids loved working with Pete. One of the Our Gang stars, Jackie Cooper, said: 'To stay a whole weekend with Pete…was my idea of glory and paradise combined.'

Petey's a precise actor, with great timing.

 Put a ring on it: Pal had had a natural ring around most of his right eye, topped up with dye. For Petey it had to be drawn on – legend has it that makeup artist Max Factor himself drew the ring. When other dogs were used you can see the ring switch from right to left eyes.

 Nanny cam: Pit bulls were popular family dogs in the era and considered 'nanny dogs'.

George
Bringing Up Baby, 1938

Breed: Wire Fox Terrier

It takes a pretty special performance to steal the show from Katharine Hepburn, Cary Grant (in a maribou-trimmed ladies' dressing gown, no less) and a Victrola-loving leopard named Baby. Asta was just the dog to win over audiences playing George in Howard Hawks' witty screwball comedy about a carefree young woman 'helping' a straitlaced palaeontologist secure a big donation from her wealthy aunt (who happens to be leopard-sitting).

From the age of six months, Skippy was trained by his owners Henry East and Gale Henry East. He first came to fame starring as the pet dog Asta in *The Thin Man* movies and had already appeared with Grant in 1937's *The Awful Truth*. Skippy was later renamed Asta because of his celebrity in *The Thin Man* films.

Asta is still regarded as one of the best canine actors ever. Asta is still regarded as one of the best canine actors ever, and in *Bringing Up Baby* he demonstrates brilliant barking timing, a range of facial expressions, dashing away with a priceless dinosaur bone, diligently digging holes across a 26-acre garden, singing along to 'I Can't Give You Anything But Love, Baby', and holding his own in a playful sparring session with Baby the leopard.

 A real pro: At the height of his fame, Asta could earn $250 a week while his trainer earned just $60. Other actors weren't allowed to talk to him between takes because his owners thought it would break his concentration, and he had his own dressing room.

 Heavy petting: Animal lover Katharine Hepburn enjoyed petting the leopard on set; Cary Grant was more fond of the safer interactions with Asta.

Toto
The Wizard of Oz, 1939

Breed: Cairn Terrier

Oz might not exist without Toto. Kansas farmgirl Dorothy would have never run out into that tornado if she hadn't been trying to protect her beloved pooch. Toto is in nearly every scene of this classic, from the opening serenade of 'Over the Rainbow' to the emotional 'there's no place like home' finale. It's Toto who rounds up the Scarecrow, Tin Man and Cowardly Lion to rescue Dorothy; it's Toto who ventures behind the curtain to expose the Wizard.

Terry was scared of the wind machines and startled by the steam that came out of the Tin Man's hat.

MGM had famously considered a man in a dog suit to play Toto; it's hard to imagine that scenario after seeing legendary terrier Terry play the role.

Trainer Carl Spitz adopted Terry as a shy, meek one-year-old and brought her out of her shell. Terry still had some spooked moments on set, as she was scared of the wind machines and startled by the steam that came out of the Tin Man's hat. But Terry's friendship with Judy Garland bolstered the pooch after a mishap: the dog suffered a sprained foot when accidentally stepped on by one of the Wicked Witch's guardsmen. Terry took two weeks off the shoot and spent recovery time at Garland's house. Terry, you're not in Kansas anymore.

 Pup's paycheck: Spitz was paid $125 per week for Terry's services – not as much as Judy Garland's $500 a week, but more than the $50 a week some of the Munchkins earned.

 What's in a name: Terry starred in 16 films, but Oz became so iconic that Spitz later changed the dog's name to Toto.

Lassie

Lassie Come Home, 1943

Breed: Rough Collie

Lassie was an overnight success: the most famous dog in history was a star straight from this first hit film.

Adapted from Eric Knight's novel, *Lassie Come Home* is a simple but moving story about Yorkshire lad Joe (Roddy McDowall) and his loyal and intelligent collie. Joe's impoverished family has to sell the dog and Lassie is taken to his new owner in Scotland (where she meets Priscilla, played by 11-year-old Elizabeth Taylor). But the dog is so loyal to Joe that she is determined to undertake a perilous journey of several hundred miles to get home.

A male one-year-old collie named Pal – owned and trained by Rudd Weatherwax – was originally cast as a lowly stunt dog, but was promoted to the lead

One critic called Lassie 'Greer Garson with fur'.

after he adroitly navigated a tricky river scene. As director Fred M. Wilcox claimed, 'Pal jumped into that water, and Lassie climbed out!' He was also skilled at jumping fences, walking with a limp or crashing through a windowpane.

Pal starred in six more MGM films and the two pilots for the 1950s TV show before retiring. One critic called Lassie 'Greer Garson with fur' and the dog also inspired a financial windfall, grossing $238 million for MGM in the 1940s.

 Big fur: Pal's long, thick coat shed less in the summer than the female collie originally cast in the role. That lustrous fur also helped conceal the canine actor's manhood!

 Leading lady: For her 60th birthday, Elizabeth Taylor was given a collie puppy that was a great-grandchild (seven generations back) of Pal.

Flike

Umberto D, 1952

Breed: Terrier Mix

Even Italian neorealist master Vittorio De Sica knew the power of a dog on screen. *Umberto D* – which is considered by some critics to be an even finer film than De Sica's Oscar-winning *Bicycle Thieves* – demonstrates just how important the human–canine relationship is with its moving portrayal of a struggling retired civil servant and his trusty terrier.

As the old man battles debt and a demanding landlady, Flike is beside him (most often curled up at the foot of his single bed). And when man's best friend goes missing, Umberto's panic is palpable.

As Umberto describes him, Flike is 'a mutt with intelligent eyes, white with brown spots' and he's also 'impossible to hate'. Agreed. When things get especially desperate, it's Flike who gives Umberto a reason to keep on living.

De Sica used a mostly non-professional cast for the film: Umberto himself was played by a professor named Carlo Battisti. But the dog actor, Napoleone, was a trained professional.

Flike is 'a mutt with intelligent eyes, white with brown spots' and he's also 'impossible to hate'.

Napoleone's most impressive stunt is standing or walking on his hind legs – he even learns to beg for money by holding Umberto's hat in his mouth, in a scene shot outside the Pantheon in Rome.

 Fun and games: Carlo Battisti and Napoleone bonded on set so that the dog would play hide and seek with him in the film's pivotal final scenes.

 French dip: The film was remade in 2008 as *Un homme et son chien,* starring Jean-Paul Belmondo and a five-year-old terrier mix named Clap.

Yeller

Old Yeller, 1957

Breed: Yellow Labrador/Mastiff Mix

Yeller is a stray dog taken in by the Coates family on their 1860s Texas farm; he helps protect mom and sons Travis and Arliss while dad is away on a cattle drive. Yeller is a great companion for the boys as well as a guard dog fighting off a bear, wild boars and a wolf to keep the family safe. So that makes the film all the more tear-jerking when Yeller contracts rabies and…well, just keep a box of tissues handy.

Spike, a rescue dog thought to be part yellow Labrador/part mastiff, was bought by famed animal trainers Frank and Rudd Weatherwax for $3. He won the role of Yeller because of his look and huge stature (weighing in at 160 pounds). His lop ear became a signature.

> **Spike wasn't just a tough physical performer, he had a very attentive face.**

Spike wasn't just a tough physical performer, he had a very attentive face and could show emotion in quieter scenes.

Kevin Corcoran, who played younger brother Arliss, remembered, 'He was a bright, gentle animal. He was on another plane of intelligence, this dog knew what we were saying to him.'

The folksy theme song to this enduring Disney family classic was right, Yeller was the 'best doggone dog in the West'. Pass the tissues.

 Cooling down: Spike had his own trailer on the set, not just as a luxury but also to keep him cool in the California heat so that his tongue wouldn't be hanging out in close-ups.

 Gentle giant: Walt Disney almost didn't cast Spike because he thought the dog was too easygoing after being raised around children. So Frank Weatherwax had to train him for weeks to convince Disney that Spike could look vicious for the end of the film.

Bobby

Greyfriars Bobby: The True Story of a Dog, 1961

Breed: Skye Terrier

This Disney classic is based on the tear-jerking true story of a Skye terrier who lived in 19th-century Edinburgh and loyally guarded the grave of his master Old Jock for 14 years after his death.

The story isn't as dour as it sounds – Bobby himself is a jolly fellow, scampering around town to visit his many friends and collect tasty treats. Even Old Jock's final hours with Bobby give the perky pup the chance to show off a series of talented tricks: 'beg for your supper', 'down', 'up', and errr…'die for your country'.

Walt Disney, a dog lover himself, was keen to adapt Eleanor Atkinson's 1912 novel, inspired by the legend of Bobby, and held open auditions for 'a ball of fur the size of a lady's muff'. Disney scouts found the right terrier from Stornoway, and the dog was promptly renamed Bobby, insured for £20,000 and given his own caravan.

Disney scouts found the right terrier from Stornoway.

Bobby's story was retold in a 2006 film (which scandalously cast a West Highland terrier) but the 1961 version remains definitive, thanks especially to that 'bonnie wee thing': the cheeky, photogenic Bobby.

 Playing dead: In the scene when Bobby needs to trail Old Jock's coffin to Greyfriars, dog trainer John Darlys was hidden inside the coffin so the dog would follow behind.

 Bronze beauty: There is a life-size bronze sculpture honoring the real Bobby in Edinburgh, and the Museum of Edinburgh displays his collar and bowl.

Red

Big Red, 1962

Breed: Irish Setter

The first thing to know about this film is that it features a boy carrying a backpack full of puppies. Yes, a backpack full of puppies. Why isn't there an Oscar category for best baby animals in hand luggage?

The boy with the backpack is an orphan in Quebec named Rene, who is helping a rich owner take care of his show dogs, in particular the gorgeous Irish setter Red.

Rene and the dog develop such a close bond that Red injures himself jumping through a window to be with the boy. His show days may be over after that, but the dog still gets to demonstrate his heroic side by protecting his pregnant mate Molly and saving his stern owner from a mountain lion.

Why isn't there an Oscar category for best baby animals in hand luggage?

Scraps (full showname Champion Red Aye Scraps), from California, played Red. Veteran trainer William Koelher taught him to perform hunting, running, jumping and water sequences, as well as more sensitive, intimate scenes.

Scraps' coat has a magnificent sheen on screen, and get a look at that long tongue hanging out the side of his mouth. Plus…a backpack full of puppies!

 They call it puppy love: More than 60 puppies were used during the 10-month shoot; Haleridge Princess Cenna, who played mama dog Molly, was encouraged to lick the pups on cue when they were coated with food.

 Big career: Big Red's trainer William Koelher worked with 25,000 dogs during his 50-year career; he worked for Walt Disney for more than 20 years.

Sounder

Sounder, 1972

Breed: Redbone Coonhound

Sounder, adapted from an award-winning book, is the moving story of a poor sharecropping family in rural Louisiana during the Great Depression. Sounder is the family's talented hunting dog – particularly attached to teenager David Lee. Sounder certainly lives up to his name: he has a bark heard all around Louisiana, until he's shot by a policeman and runs away. The hound is reunited with David Lee but has lost his bark.

> **Sounder certainly lives up to his name: he has a bark heard all around Louisiana.**

Sounder is a strong hunter (he helps the poor family to track animals like raccoons for food) and he protects David on an epic journey to find his dad at a labour camp.

The main canine actor, a Redbone coonhound – the same breed seen in *Where the Red Fern Grows* – is a handsome hound with floppy ears, and a tongue lolling out the side of his mouth.

This is a dog film with real pedigree: Paul Winfield and Cecily Tyson were Oscar-nominated for their roles.

Sounder movingly explores themes like family ties, parental sacrifice, hard work, the importance of education, and, of course, the loyalty of a dog. As the dad proudly says, 'Ain't no dog as good as Sounder.'

 Top trainer: The dogs used in the film were trained by veteran Frank Weatherwax, who also worked with Lassie and Old Yeller.

 Deja vu: Kevin Hooks, who played David Lee in the original film, directed a *Sounder* remake in 2003. This starred Paul Winfield, who played the father in the original film, as the teacher.

Digby
Digby: The Biggest Dog in the World, 1973

Breed: Old English Sheepdog

Hey, kids, gather round and see how bad special effects were in the 1970s! This achingly British family film is a classic of a certain era, and very dated now – the camp tone is like a *Carry On* film without the smut – but still a fun watch for nostalgic adults or young kids.

Billy (Richard Beaumont) adopts a sheepdog from a shelter but has to give him to his neighbour, Jeff (Jim Dale), who happens to be working on a top secret government experiment, Project X. When Digby accidentally drinks a Project X potion, he grows to the size of a horse, then to the size of a lorry, then to the size of King Kong. Billy and Jeff have to hope that an antidote will work, or the military will obliterate Digby.

See how bad special effects were in the 1970s.

The canine actor is Fernville Lord Digby, aged three at the time, a pedigreed Old English sheepdog who also modelled for the famous Dulux paint advertisements.

Even when Digby is normal sized, he's transfixing to watch as his white and grey shaggy coat swishes around (of course obscuring his eyes and most of his facial expressions). You'll be humming the *Digby* theme song for days.

 Welcome to the dollhouse: Fernville Lord Digby shot some of his 'giant' scenes with dollhouse-sized furniture.

 Joy of painting: In a nod to Fernville Lord Digby's other job as Dulux spokesdog, you can spot a can of Dulux paint in the film as Jeff paints the dog flap.

Old Dan & Little Ann

Where the Red Fern Grows, 1974

Breed: Redbone Coonhound

Adapted from the award-winning 1961 novel, *Where the Red Fern Grows* is a moving story about a boy's coming of age in the Ozarks during the Great Depression. Stewart Peterson plays 12-year-old Billy Colman, who is obsessed with raccoon hunting but can't afford hunting dogs. So he saves up all his pocket money to buy his dream puppies, which he names Old Dan and Little Ann. He and his younger sisters train them to be highly skilled raccoon hunters, soon good enough to be competing in a local championship.

Old Dan and Little Ann's red, glossy coats shine on screen. In all, 16 dogs played the pair from puppies to adulthood. Rowdy and Blue, from Sacramento, California, starred as the mature Dan and Ann. They were trained and handled by Harold 'Butch' Packer, George Kerr and Gerry Warshauer, who had been an apprentice of Frank Inn of *Benji* fame.

The hounds work well as pairs, sharing a sack as puppies, or bolting through the woods to chase raccoons up a tree. In a more placid performance, Blue's graveside scene was the hardest to film, requiring about 12 takes to get it right.

Old Dan and Little Ann's red, glossy coats shine on screen, and their howls are meant to be experienced in surround sound…unless you are a raccoon.

 Puppy tale: Sequel *Where the Red Fern Grows: Part 2* is about Billy returning home as a World War II veteran and raising two new puppies.

 Hands on: Rowdy and Blue did a tour of Oklahoma schools to promote the film; California-based trainer George Kerr joked that they 'almost had all the hair petted off them'.

Benji

Benji, 1974

Breed: Mixed Breed

Benji wasn't just a dog, he was a cultural phenomenon. This shaggy mixed-breed mutt became an icon in the 1970s thanks to Joe Camp's underdog of a film that became a blockbuster loved by millions.

The titular tyke really is the star of this family classic. He announces himself in an ambling opening sequence by climbing over rooftops and jaunting through a small Texas town, truly a dog making his own way in the world. Love blossoms between Benji and Tiffany the Maltese, and of course Benji rescues his favourite kids Cindy and Paul by stealing a ransom note pivotal to stopping the film's preposterous kidnapping plot.

The scenes of Benji scampering through soft-focus daffodils seem dated now, but the dog's point-of-view filmmaking was groundbreaking at the time. The canine performance is one for the ages, thanks to especially fine work by rescue dog Higgins.

Higgins was special because of the range of emotions he could display on cue. Famed animal expert Frank Inn taught Higgins more than 100 tricks. But the dog, who was practically elderly at 14 when the film shot, was even more special because of the range of emotions he could display on cue: content, inquisitive, distressed, sad. No wonder millions fell in love with him.

 Not for the birds: The film was a guilty pleasure for Alfred Hitchcock.

 Daddy's girl: Higgins' daughter, Benjean, took over the role of Benji in the first two film sequels.

Sandy

Annie, 1982

Breed: Otterhound

In this starry musical, the famous orphan meets street dog Sandy when she rescues him from a pack of mean boys. Annie's cunning also saves Sandy from the dogcatcher, after which she takes him home to the orphanage. She loves the mutt so much that when she is offered the chance to move to billionaire Daddy Warbucks' mansion, she won't go without her hound. On a fancy trip to Radio City Music Hall, the shaggy sidekick even gets his own velvet seat.

'That old belief that you should beware of children and animals is absurd.'

The lead canine actor was six-year-old Bingo, a pedigree otterhound (a rare British breed), who dined every night of the shoot on steak or prime rib. Sandy doesn't have many challenging stunts in the film – except jumping into a pool to 'save' Daddy Warbucks – but he impresses with his natural charm, like when hiding under a pile of laundry and being serenaded by dozens of little girls.

John Huston, the veteran filmmaker behind *The Maltese Falcon* who was improbably hired to direct *Annie*, came around to working with Bingo…and dozens of dancing kids. He said, 'that old belief that you should beware of children and animals is absurd. If you know anything about children and animals, they live up to your expectations, always.'

 Fruity fun: To entice Bingo to kiss her when needed, Aileen Quinn, the 10-year-old actress who played Annie, would rub an apple on her face.

 Remake revisions: The 2014 remake of *Annie* saw Sandy played by a completely different kind of dog – Marti, a golden retriever-chow mix rescued from a shelter.

White dog

White Dog, 1982

Breed: German Shepherd

Samuel Fuller's *White Dog* isn't an easy watch, as it tackles the serious subject of racism. The shepherd is not just a 'white dog' in its appearance, the term also describes a dog trained by a racist white owner to attack black people.

When a young actress, Julie (Kirsty McNichol), rescues such a dog, she learns his dark secret and takes him to movie animal training experts to be 'reprogrammed'.

> **It's like a well-choreographed dance watching the dog in the ring with determined trainer Keys.**

It took four dogs to play the challenging part: Folsom, Heinz, Buster and Duke. Famed trainer Karl Lewis Miller was in charge of the physically demanding animal action, which sees the dog pacing around a cage, tackling his subjects, climbing out of his compound, and even leaping over a chain-link fence. And watching the dog in the ring with determined trainer Keys (Paul Winfield) is like observing a well-choreographed dance.

Miller said, '[Fuller] didn't want to show a dog that looked trained, where the dog is in the centre of a scene and you know that it's looking at a trainer beside the camera telling him what to do. This really led me to pinpoint my own specialty in this business, and that is training dogs to look untrained.'

 Colour blind: Fuller had wanted a black German shepherd to play the dog, but one studio executive had taken the title literally and asked Karl Lewis Miller to start training white German shepherds.

 Animal lover: Fuller was so concerned about not hurting any animals that he moved the location of one shot after finding a mouse nest there.

Cujo
Cujo, 1983

Breed: Saint Bernard

Macabre master Stephen King wouldn't write a sweet story about a mild-mannered mutt, would he? There are ominous signals about Cujo's future from the very first scene, as the Saint Bernard chases a rabbit into a cave inhabited by bats. And thus begins Cujo's transformation from affectionate to rabid. Put down the popcorn and steady yourself for screams and slobber.

In a classic siege story, mom Donna (Dee Wallace) and her son Tad (Danny Pintauro) are trapped in their broken-down car as Cujo becomes more and more aggressive. He's a fearsome, battering

The canine actors were so playful and happy during the attack scenes that their wagging tails had to be tied down with fishing line.

beast – foaming at the mouth (egg whites and sugar), covered in blood (red-dyed syrup) and with a crazed look in his eyes.

It took five dogs, a mechanical head, and a stuntman in a dog suit to play the multi-faceted role of Cujo. The canine actors were so playful and happy during the attack scenes that their wagging tails had to be tied down with fishing line.

Teresa Ann Miller, animal trainer and daughter of Cujo trainer Karl Lewis Miller, remembers one of the Cujo dogs, Daddy, living with her family and being 'very sweet', which made the dog's hair-raising performance in the film all the more impressive.

 Toy time: For the scenes of Cujo attacking the car, the filmmakers hid the dogs' favourite toys inside the vehicle so they would try to jump in.

 Hog dog: Stephen King said he was inspired to write the story after meeting his motorcycle mechanic's menacing dog.

Matisse

Down and Out in Beverly Hills, 1986

Breed: Border Collie

It's not easy living in the lap of luxury. Matisse, cinema's most neurotic canine character, is pampered in his Beverly Hills mansion. But he's unhappy and refuses to eat. Owner Barbara Whiteman (Bette Midler) hires a wacky dog psychologist to diagnose him. Dr. Von Zimmer's verdict? 'Hug the dog, he needs reassurance. He suffers from nipple anxiety, he probably came from a nine-dog litter.'

Mike was famed for his one blue eye and one floppy ear.

The unexpected cure comes when a homeless man, Jerry (Nick Nolte), is 'adopted' by the family patriarch, Dave Whiteman (Richard Dreyfuss). Hanging out with Jerry, Matisse is finally able to eat (Jerry bends down and shares a bowl of puppy chow with him).

Matisse was played with aplomb by Mike, a dog trained by Clint Rowe. Famed for his one blue eye and one floppy ear, Mike makes a perfect paw-over-the-eyes move in the scene where Nick Nolte strips naked by the pool.

Mike had humble beginnings – Rowe discovered him chained up at a ranch in Northern California and the pup had to spend seven weeks in a cast when he was kicked by a horse. Rowe later taught him more than 100 tricks. Scene stealing was just one of them.

 Career ladder: Mike landed the role after showing director Paul Mazursky that he could climb a rope ladder with a bucket in his mouth.

 Bad taste: Legend has it that Nick Nolte ate real dog food while shooting the film.

Hooch

Turner & Hooch, 1989

Breed: Dogue de Bordeaux

Hooch is the original lovable bad dog in film – think of him as the ur-Marley or Beethoven.

Hooch is the witness to a murder, so uptight police investigator Scott Turner (Tom Hanks) teams up with the dog to solve the crime. Don't dwell on the ridiculous plot – focus on the magical relationship between young Hanks and his slobbering and slovenly sidekick.

Hooch on his own manages one of the film's best scenes, when he thoroughly trashes Turner's flat.

A 10-year-old chocolate brown Dogue de Bordeaux (a rare breed) named Beasley took the lead, trained by Clint Rowe. Three other Dogues – Barry, Vigor and Cristo – were doubles.

Beasley manages one of the film's best scenes when he thoroughly trashes Turner's flat: devouring popcorn, spraying slobber over the hi-fi and vinyl collection, destroying the sofa and even chugging a few beers. When he's caught in the act, the guilty look on Hooch's face, with his head on Turner's pillow, is priceless.

Turner and Hooch make one of cinema's best odd couples. No wonder Hanks later said he wished the script had an, ahem, different ending for Hooch. Hanks would have been consoled to know there was at least a happy ending for Beasley. Most Dogues only live to age six but he lived to the ripe old age of 14 – or 98 in dog years. That's a lot of slobber.

 Daylight slobbery: Egg whites were used to create the copious amounts of on-screen slobber. One of the hardest tasks to train Beasley for was to shake his head on cue so that the slobber sprayed everywhere.

 Soup's on: Beasley didn't want to drink beer, so he drank cans of chicken soup instead.

Jerry Lee
K-9, 1989

Breed: German Shepherd

Michael Dooley (Jim Belushi) is a San Diego narcotics officer who needs a new partner. Enter the smelly, chilli-eating German shepherd named Jerry Lee (after 'the Killer', Jerry Lee Lewis).

Jerry Lee is one skilled animal – he bites through pool balls, he attacks bad guys, he sips iced tea by the beach, he leaps between rooftops (actually filmed only 3 feet off the ground), he bounds into a moving truck, he survives a gunshot wound, and he even bags a pretty poodle for himself.

Dooley starts out without an appreciation for dogs – he even claims not to have cried watching the end of *Old Yeller* (sacrilege!) – but

Four dogs from Germany who were already training to become police dogs shared the lead role.

Jerry Lee lures him in and by the end Dooley says, 'He's not just a dog. He's a cop. He's not just any cop, he's my partner.'

In some great typecasting, four dogs originally from Germany who were already training to become police dogs shared the lead role. Animal trainer Karl Lewis Miller explained that the regal Rando had special skills. 'The typical dog knows 10 or 15 commands, but Rando has anywhere from 125 to 150 actions,' Miller said. Trainer Teresa Ann Miller, who also worked on the film, remembers Rando as 'a really loving dog, a funny dog, just like the character'.

 Behind the scenes: The scene where Jerry Lee goes through the car wash wasn't faked – the trainer had to make sure special soaps were used so the dog's coat and eyes weren't irritated.

 Buddy picture: Jim Belushi loved working with Rando. Belushi said, 'He'd come on the set, steal all the women's attention, steal the scene and walk away to his trailer when he was done. No hellos, no thank-yous, no goodbyes. He's a real Errol Flynn.'

White Fang
White Fang, 1991

Breed: Wolfdog

White Fang's story unfolds alongside a young Gold Rush prospector named Jack, and the wolfdog's life is often more interesting than Jack's. As a puppy, he is orphaned and has to fend for himself without a pack in the Alaskan wilderness; he's adopted by a Native American family who train him to work, then he gets nabbed by professional dog fighters. When White Fang is injured in a brawl, Jack nurses him back to health and teaches him to trust humans again.

White Fang is quite the hero – he saves Jack from a bear, from a mine cave-in, and from a fire in his cabin. He's even the one who discovers gold on Jack's land.

Clint Rowe owned and trained lead dog Jed, who was part wolf (some sources say about 25%) and part Alaskan malamute.

If I were teaching an acting class, I'd get the half-wolf from *White Fang* to come in.

Both Jed and lead actor Ethan Hawke more than do justice to Jack London's 1906 classic adventure novel. Hawke, who was just 20 when he made the film, has paid tribute to Jed for decades. '[Jed] was one of the best actors I ever worked with…I'd see the way the wolf reacted to the camera when someone came into the room. Acting surprised. Not expecting it. If I were teaching an acting class, I'd get the half-wolf from *White Fang* to come in.'

Showing the fangs: To get Jed to growl and show a savage look by bearing his fangs, his trainer Clint Rowe simply said 'teeth'.

Play fight: In the scene where White Fang is attacked by a pit bull, Jed wore a fur collar. That's what the pit bull is biting, not Jed's neck.

Beethoven

Beethoven, 1992

Breed: Saint Bernard

Size does matter in this hit franchise. Beethoven, the lovable, bumbling, drooling Saint Bernard, weighs in at 185 pounds at his beefy best.

As a nameless puppy, he escapes from dognappers and sneaks into the home of the Newton family, led by grumpy dad Charles Grodin. Beethoven – christened because of his unexpected appreciation of the com-

Chris wanted attention but he wasn't a big cuddler.

poser's Fifth Symphony – soon wreaks household havoc: he pees in dad's brief-case and drools on his trousers, snatches bacon off the dining table, and drinks out of the fish bowl. More helpfully, he saves one of the Newton daughters from drowning, and helps another meet the boy of her dreams. In return, the family saves their hefty hound from an evil vet.

Chris played Beethoven, aided by a mechanical dog for some stunts. It's hilarious seeing Chris spooning with George Newton in bed, or getting his leash tangled in a table and chairs, dragging George's helpless business clients down the street.

Animal trainer Teresa Ann Miller, whose father Karl Lewis Miller was in charge of Beethoven, remembers Chris as 'a beautiful, strong independent guy. He wanted attention but he wasn't a big cuddler.' It's probably safer that way: 185 pounds is a lot of cuddle.

 Pool cool: For the scene when Beethoven saves Emily in the pool and she rides him to safety, a man in a dog suit was used.

 Triple threat: Chris played Beethoven in the first two movies. After his death it took three dogs (Benz, Dolly and Boomer) to take on the role in the other six sequels.

Chance

Homeward Bound: The Incredible Journey, 1993

Breed: American Bulldog

Young bulldog Chance is adopted into a happy family that also includes Himalayan cat Sassy (whose catchphrase is 'dogs drool and cats rule') and wise old golden retriever Shadow. The pets are sent to a farm (not a euphemism) while their human family temporarily moves to a small apartment.

Shadow encourages Chance and Sassy to embark on an epic, and perilous, journey back home, even crossing the Sierra Nevada mountains. Along the way, Chance learns how important his humans and his home are.

It's wonderful to see the animals getting more screen time than the humans.

It's wonderful to see the animals getting more screen time than the humans; they speak to each other (and are voiced by greats Michael J. Fox, Sally Field and Don Ameche) but without any distracting mouth movements. In Disney's 1963 version of the same story, which featured different breeds, the animals' thoughts were narrated instead.

A total of four dogs played Chance, with purebred Rattler playing most of the role.

Watching the cat and dogs cross these gorgeous vistas, you start to believe they actually are cross-species comrades – and they did really become friends. Dog trainer Gary 'Sam' Vaughn said, 'Our animals spent so much time together that they have become very close.'

 The dog that takes the cream: In the scene where Chance plunges his head into a wedding cake, the canine actor loved whipped cream so much that the filmmakers spread cream on him so he wouldn't eat too much.

 Feeding frenzy: The felines playing Sassy were encouraged to lick the dogs' faces, thanks to some strategically applied cat food.

Yellow

Far From Home: The Adventures of Yellow Dog, 1995

Breed: Labrador Retriever

It's hard to decide what's more beautiful, Yellow the Labrador retriever or the gorgeous scenery of British Columbia. Both get plenty of screen time in *Far From Home*, a family-friendly adventure story about a teenage boy, Angus (Jesse Bradford), who finds a Lab and names him Yellow. When Angus runs into a disaster on a sailing trip, he and Yellow have to stick together to survive in the wilderness, facing cold, rain, hunger, exhaustion and even wild beasts like a wolf and a lynx.

> **It's hard to decide what's more beautiful, Yellow the Labrador retriever or the gorgeous scenery of British Columbia.**

Five Labs played Yellow, led by Dakotah, with some help from Schroeder, Auggie, Foster and Linus. An animatronic dog was also used for some perilous scenes (such as Yellow's fall from a great height into fast-flowing water). The dogs really did film a scene on girders spanning a 150-foot gorge; they had safety lines attached at all times.

Labs are already comfortable in water, and Foster trained for weeks to swim with the raft in a river.

This boy and his dog have a special bond in the story, and it plays out gorgeously on screen, thanks to a special bond between actor Jesse Bradford and Dakotah.

 Digging for treasure: In a scene where Angus teaches Yellow to dig for clams in the sand, Dakotah was digging for buried dog treats.

 Too nice: Dakotah was so nice that the wolf wouldn't growl at him, and an Airedale mix had to stand in for that scene.

Fly

Babe, 1995

Breed: Border Collie

No doubt, *Babe* is the finest talking-animal movie ever made, and maybe even the finest animal movie ever. Its numbers are impressive: 970 trained animals, 57 animal handlers, 18 months of animal training, six months of filming and 12 months of post-production. All that helped to rake in $250 million at the box office and earn seven Oscar nominations (including one win for visual effects).

The pigs and dogs all bonded playing during weeks of pre-production.

As in Dick King-Smith's 1983 book on which the film is based, when an orphaned pig arrives at Hoggett's farm, Fly the sheepdog becomes his adoptive mother. On his first night at the farm, she puts her paw on Babe's little head and they are inseparable ever after. She gives Babe's face a grateful lick when he calls her 'Mom' for the first time, and despite her mate Rex's ego-driven objections, Fly helps Babe become an unlikely sheepherder.

Fly (voiced by the jolly Miriam Margolyes) is good at dashing around the sheep as well as delivering emotions – looking confused, concentrating or looking forlorn (like when her pups are taken away). The snuggly chemistry was real between the dozens of pigs that played Babe and the several dogs who played Fly – they had all bonded playing during weeks of pre-production. That'll do, pig (and dog).

 Reality bites: About 80% of the film was made with real animals, and 20% using animatronic creatures. Digital computer animation was added to help them 'talk' in post-production.

 Puppy love: Veteran animal trainer Karl Lewis Miller supervised all the animals and handlers and also had a small role, playing the happy man who buys Fly's puppies.

The puppies
101 Dalmations, 1996

Breed: Dalmation

After the 1961 animated classic, Disney brought this beloved story to the big screen in live action in 1996, complete with real dogs and one intimidating bitch: Cruella de Vil, played by Glenn Close.

Canine couple Pongo and Perdy are brought together when their owners fall in love. They have a litter of 15 adorable puppies who are dognapped, along with 84 other puppies, because Cruella wants them for a fiendish fur coat.

At eight weeks old the 230 puppies were brought to the set, and there were 13 trainers to work with them.

The production used 230 puppies and 20 adult dogs. All of the puppies came from private homes as entire litters. Owners started training the dogs at six weeks old; at eight weeks old they were brought to the set at Shepperton Studios in the UK, working with 13 trainers.

There are six 'hero' puppies: Wizzer, distinguishable by his two black ears; Two-tone, by the one black ear; the densely spotted Lucky; Dipstick, aptly named because of his black tail; Jewel, with her 'necklace' of spots; and Fidget, who has one blue eye.

Health and safety measures were crucial with so many vulnerable young animals, and the set was disinfected daily. Head animal trainer Gary Gero explained, 'No one has ever worked with puppies on this scale.'

 Newborn nerves: The pivotal scene with Lucky coming to life stars a puppy who was just three days old (it was swaddled in a disinfected blanket). Only Jeff Daniels and the dog's owner touched the dog.

 Voicing concerns: Glenn Close, an avowed dog lover, said her Cruella voice could frighten the dogs. 'Little Perdy would slink off the set with her tail between her legs. I felt very bad.'

Buddy
Air Bud, 1997

Breed: Golden Retriever

That's not CGI wizardry, Buddy the golden retriever really can play basketball. The initial thought is, 'This can't be real'. That's why the film's end credits point out emphatically that 'no special visual effects were used in the basketball sequences'.

The story is simple – Buddy runs away from an abusive clown and is adopted by a lonely teenage boy, Josh, who breaks out of his shell thanks to Buddy's companionship (and also his dexterity on the basketball court).

Owner Kevin DiCicco found Buddy as a stray dog wandering out of the forest in the Sierra Nevada mountains, and played

Buddy the golden retriever really can play basketball.

catch with him to nurse him back to health. DiCicco realized Buddy had special sporting skills and trained him to play basketball (his favourite), baseball, American football, soccer and hockey.

After Buddy dunked a ball on David Letterman's talk show, and then played Comet on TV's *Full House*, DeCicco developed the idea of the Air Bud character, which inspired five films and the Air Buddies spinoffs.

Hoops aren't Buddy's only skills in the film; he's also confident climbing a trellis, walking across a roof, and jumping into a bedroom window. He delivered on the film's genius tagline: 'He sits. He stays. He shoots. He scores.'

 By the number: Buddy's basketball jersey features the number K-9.

 Well oiled: The basketballs that Buddy used were partially deflated and coated with olive oil to make them easier for him to handle.

Zeus

Zeus and Roxanne, 1997

Breed: Portuguese Podengo

Zeus has the finest quizzical head tilt in the business. It's especially charming when the appealingly scrappy, skinny Portuguese Podengo cocks his head as he starts communicating with a dolphin.

In Florida, a widowed composer, his son and their dog Zeus move next door to a marine biologist and her two daughters. The kids scheme, *Parent Trap*-style, to get their parents together, but the most important relationship that develops is an amazing inter-species friendship between Zeus and Roxanne the dolphin.

This maritime mutt is especially good in and around water, laying on and leaping from boats.

Zeus was played by three dogs – Nikki, Tito and Rosa – all wire-haired Portuguese Podengos, a lively and intelligent breed that was formerly known for rabbit hunting.

This maritime mutt is especially good in and around water, laying on and leaping from boats (and even 'steering' a boat at one point).

There is a look of genuine happiness on Zeus' face when he's around Roxanne (who is an impressively twirling performer herself). The human dialogue can be cringeworthy – 'If a dog and a dolphin can get along, why not our mom and his dad?' – but all is forgiven, thanks to a stunning scene when Zeus hitches a ride on Roxanne's back.

 Surf's up: The scene in which Zeus rides on Roxanne's back was shot with a real dog but an animatronic dolphin; it's still an impressive feat because getting a pooch to surf atop a robotic animal also isn't easy!

 In demand: Nikki, Tito and Rosa also acted in *Homeward Bound 2, Cheaper by the Dozen, Monster-in-Law* and *The Lake House.*

Verdell
As Good As It Gets, 1997

Breed: Brussels Griffon

A very important life lesson emerges in *As Good As It Gets*: bacon equals love. Or at the very least, you can win a dog's love with a pocketful of cured meats.

The whole cast and crew was 'oohing and aahing' over her.

Curmudgeonly author Melvin Udall (Jack Nicholson won an Oscar for the role) learns this trick when he has to unexpectedly dogsit Verdell, who belongs to his neighbour Simon (Greg Kinnear). Melvin doesn't much like Verdell – he puts him down the garbage chute and refuses to touch him without wearing plastic gloves. But soon the grumpy, OCD-suffering Melvin warms to Verdell and he serenades the dog with 'Always Look on the Bright Side of Life'.

Six Brussels griffons (a rare but intelligent toy breed) played Verdell: Timer, Sprout, Debbie, Billy, Parfait and Jill. Texas-born Jill (trained by Mathilde de Cagny) was singled out as the smartest and prettiest, and got the most screen time.

De Cagny found Jill when a breeder rejected her because she wouldn't make a good show dog. But de Cagny said she was 'the prettiest girl ever…amazing, super adorable, charming. The whole cast and crew was "oohing and aahing" over her.'

 Two faces of Jack: Jill had a complicated relationship with Jack Nicholson. They were buddies between takes, but because his character is supposed to hate the dog initially, Jill would get confused by her friend Jack being mean to her in a scene.

 Alive and kicking: In a scene when Verdell gets 'kicked', Jill was trained to rest on Jack's foot and then pop up at the right time.

Puffy
There's Something About Mary, 1998

Breed: Border Terrier

This Farrelly Brothers' raucous comedy boasts three iconic images: the stuck zipper, the 'hair gel' and poor Puffy in a body cast.

> **Puffy lunges for Ted's face, and then for his ankle, and finally his groin, in full-on attack mode.**

Even with its raunchy moments, this is a sweet story at its core, about a geek, Ted (Ben Stiller), who botched his prom date with a beautiful girl, Mary (Cameron Diaz), and 13 years later wants to win her back.

One way to Mary's heart is through her neighbour Magda's beloved dog, Puffy. But Puffy has already been set on fire and brought back to life by another suitor, Healy (Matt Dillon), who feeds him uppers ahead of his meeting with Ted. The jacked-up dog lunges for Ted's face, and then for his ankle, and finally his groin, in full-on attack mode. He eventually sails out the window as Ted ducks his final assault.

A female border terrier named Slammer played Puffy, and there were at least six fake Puffy dolls used in the film (such as when Healy sets Puffy on fire and Ted leaves him on the top of the car).

Another iconic moment is Puffy's French kiss with Magda. Trainer Kim Lindemoen worked with the dog extensively on the fight scene as well as the memorable lip-lock. Lindemoen said, 'When Slammer started kissing her face, she got really involved in it and wouldn't stop!'

 Cast away: The cast costume wasn't uncomfortable for Slammer – it was made of linen and loosely fitted and used quick-release velcro closures.

 Over the moon: In the scene where Puffy jumps out of the window, Bobby Farrelly didn't think the cast's expressions were shocked enough, so decided to moon them to get the right look of surprise.

Patrasche
A Dog of Flanders, 1999

Breed: Bouvier des Flandres

In this fifth film based on the classic children's novel by Ouida, Nello is a Belgian boy whose mother dies when he's a toddler, leaving him with his impoverished grandfather. He has a special place in his heart for another orphaned creature, a giant black dog who has been left for dead by his cruel owner. Nello nurses him back to health and names him Patrasche, after his mother's middle name

Patrasche bares his teeth and tackles a baddie when he needs to protect Nello.

Nello is obsessed with three things: the dog, his best friend Aloise and becoming a great artist like his idol Peter Paul Rubens. Nello has to face everything from the death of a loved one to homelessness, but the friendship of Patrasche helps him through.

Animal trainer Cindy James Cullen used three different dogs to play Patrasche at different ages. The canine actors are gentle giants (up to 120 pounds) who certainly look less awkward on screen than Jon Voight does, playing Nello's mentor and struggling with a vaguely 'European' accent.

Patrasche bares his teeth and tackles a baddie when he needs to protect Nello. He's also an excellent eater, chomping down heartily on some biscuits; and he saves the day when he sniffs out a lost wallet in the snow.

 From Texas to Belgium: In the 1959 film of the story, Spike, who also played Old Yeller, played the title role.

 Tourist trail: A statue of Nello and Patrasche can be found in front of Antwerp Cathedral.

Winky, Miss Agnes, Beatrice & Hubert

Best in Show, 2000

Breed: Norfolk Terrier, Shih Tzu, Weimaraner, Bloodhound

Best in Show is a hilarious watch for pooch parents who can laugh about their own doggy obsessions. This largely improvised comedy mockumentary by the brilliant Christopher Guest goes behind the scenes of a top dog contest (the fictional Mayflower Dog Show, inspired by the real Westminster Dog Show) as we meet impressive show dogs and their neurotic and hilarious owners.

The cast of champion canines were all played by real show dogs who knew how to perform. The cast of champion canines – Hubert the slobbering bloodhound; serenaded Norfolk terrier Winky (who inspired the song 'God Loves a Terrier'); Busy Bee-obsessed Weimaraner Beatrice and pampered shih tzu Miss Agnes – were all played by real show dogs who knew how to perform. It was the actors who needed lessons with a veteran handler, Earlene Luke, to learn how to show off these top canines.

Working with real show dogs had its perks. Director and actor Guest (of *Spinal Tap* fame) recalled, 'Considering how many dogs we have been working with, it's really remarkable how easy it's been.' Shockingly, there was only one unscripted bark in the final film (heard as two of the characters argue backstage).

 Eyes on the prize: During the research for his role, actor John Michael Higgins was asked to handle a dog at a real competition and actually won a blue ribbon.

 Ode to Winky: The genius lyrics to 'God Loves a Terrier', as sung by Winky's parents Cookie and Gerry: 'God didn't miss a stitch/be it dog or be it bitch/when he made the Norwich merrier/with his cute little 'derrier'/yes, God loves a terrier!'

Mr Beefy
Little Nicky, 2000

Breed: English Bulldog

Even the sane percentage of the population who can't abide Adam Sandler will fall in love with Mr Beefy the bulldog, his co-star in raucous comedy *Little Nicky*.

Sandler plays the son of the devil, making his first trip to Earth. Beefy the foul-mouthed bulldog (voiced by comedian Robert Smigel) becomes his unlikely chaperone around New York. The dog teaches him essential life skills like how to woo a woman and how to eat a bucket of fried chicken. What more do you need?

The role of Mr Beefy was played by three dogs trained by Steve Berens: three-year-old male Roo, seven-year-old male Harvey and two-year-old female Harley.

Berens said he enjoyed working with the dogs on some very specific shots for *Little Nicky*, 'like lifting the leg and peeing on cue, taking a dump and humping a dog in an alley'. If that's not classy enough for you, there's also a brilliant scene of Mr Beefy getting stoned and snoring on the sofa.

Sandler loved working with the dogs so much that he adopted one of Roo's

There's a brilliant scene of Mr Beefy getting stoned and snoring on the sofa.

puppies from Berens and named him Meatball. The dog, clad in a custom tuxedo, later served as the ringbearer at Sandler's wedding.

 Over the hump: The memorable scene of Beefy getting amorous with a cocker spaniel was simulated by the canine actors. Lucky was put on her mark and then Beefy was trained to put his paws on her back and simulate a humping motion.

 Hanging around: The canine actor was so comfortable in the scene in hell where he is hanging on a post with a 'wedgie', that he fell asleep and started snoring.

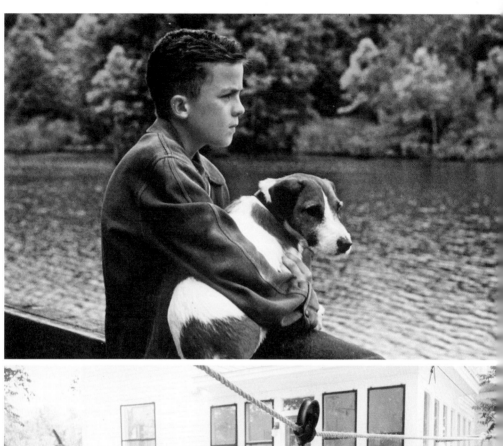

Skip
My Dog Skip, 2000

Breed: Jack Russell Terrier

Skip, the lovable Jack Russell terrier, really is a boy's best friend in this sweet tale of a lonely nine-year-old boy in a Norman Rockwell-esque town in 1940s Mississippi.

Young Willie Morris (Frankie Muniz) stands up to his bullies, woos his first girlfriend, reconnects with his father, and learns some important life lessons about war and racism thanks to Skip.

'Enzo loved toys, he loved food, he loved people, and he had a huge drive.'

Moose (best known as Eddie from TV's *Frasier*) and his son Enzo – both trained by Mathilde de Cagny – played Skip, with Enzo taking most of the scenes and Moose taking on a few shots of the elder Skip.

Enzo drinks from the toilet, jumps into Willie's arms, leaps up a tree chasing a squirrel, fights off two moonshiners in a cemetery, plays baseball and football, and even seems to drive a car. De Cagny said, 'Enzo was a dream dog. He loved toys, he loved food, he loved people, and he had a huge drive.'

It's impossible to watch Enzo, and Moose in the final scenes, and not reminisce about the first dog you ever loved.

 Playing ball: In a scene where Skip has to bound around a baseball field, the trainer showed Enzo his favourite toy, then covered his eyes. Enzo then ran around to all the kids on the field trying to find his toy.

 Family rivalry: Moose and Enzo famously couldn't be in the same room together. De Cagny explained tat this was normal with two adult male non-neutered terriers. 'It's nothing to do with egos or who does TV and movies (laughs), it's more of a dog instinct.'

Lou
Cats & Dogs, 2001

Breed: Pocket Beagle

Move over, James Bond; it's time for Goldpaw, not Goldfinger. The rivalry between canines and felines is brought to life in this fun family film about a high-tech spy war between cats and dogs to battle for world domination.

The film was shot with real dogs, with visual effects added later to make them 'talk' and puppet dogs deployed for special stunts.

Lou (voiced by Tobey Maguire), a pocket beagle, only 10 inches tall, is the standout. The script originally called for a foxhound puppy, but beagles were easier to train.

The dogs had to look like they are carrying on a normal conversation as two people would. It took five two-year-old dogs to play Lou: Buddy, Confusion, Prada, Coco and C.J. Each dog had to learn skills such as standing up, backing up, chasing their own tails, walking side by side with other dogs, licking faces, playing on command, and (gasp) working with cats. Trainer Boone Narr said, 'The hardest thing to do is have them act natural...they had to look like they are carrying on a normal conversation as two people would.'

In all, 27 dogs played Lou and his pack – including Butch the Anatolian shepherd, Ivy the Saluki, Peek the Chinese crested, and Sam the English sheepdog.

 Secret in their eyes: To get the eyelines right, Narr used 'look sticks' – a stick with a treat that would attract the dogs' eyes.

 Work and play: The dogs playing Lou did a total of more than 2,000 hours of training before the shoot started. To keep their puppy-like attitudes, the canine actors also enjoyed playtime on every training day.

Frank

Men In Black II, 2002

Breed: Pug

Is there anything better than a pug in a suit? Indeed, a talking pug in a suit.

Frank the Pug stole the show in the first *Men in Black* film with just one short scene. Thankfully he got more attention in this sequel, moving up the ranks to become Agent J's (Will Smith) sidekick, Agent F.

In both films, Mushu the pug played Frank. Since he was older in the second film, some black mascara was used to hide the grey fur around his nose.

Frank is an alien informant in a dog's body, and director Barry Sonnenfeld thought Mushu had the right look: 'He looked like an alien. He's sort of ugly and strange, and certainly not cuddly.' Pug lovers may disagree.

Frank gets more sharp chat in the sequel, as well as a chance to croon disco hit 'I Will Survive', and bark along to that canine classic 'Who Let the Dogs Out?'

Frank gets more sharp chat in the sequel, as well as a chance to croon a disco hit.

His doggy-sized MIB suit was especially stylin'. Sonnenfeld said, 'Mushu loved being in that suit, he had the best time, he just pranced around. It was like when he was in the suit he really felt like he was a man in black.'

 Learning from scratch: Mushu was a 'green dog' for the first *Men in Black*, so trainer Cristie Miele had to teach him all the basic tricks from scratch.

 Follow the leader: Sonnenfeld said, 'Will Smith was great with them (Mushu and his backup pugs).' It also meant they would hit their marks together, as Mushu was keen to follow Smith around.

Bruiser

Legally Blonde 2: Red, White & Blonde, 2003

Breed: Chihuahua

Bruiser was a fashion-forward sidekick to the effervescent law student Elle Woods (Reese Witherspoon) in the first *Legally Blonde*. As Elle graduates to become a Washington lobbyist in this sequel, Bruiser is promoted to a central character.

Bruiser inspires the whole plot – Elle is on the verge of getting married and wants to invite Bruiser's birth mother to the nuptials. A detective tracks down Bruiser's mom but discovers she's being cruelly tested on by a cosmetics company. Cue Bruiser's Bill, Elle's congressional crusade to stop animal testing.

Along the way we also find out that Bruiser is gay ('not that there's anything wrong with that', as Seinfeld would say) when he falls in love with Leslie (played by Buddy), a congressman's imposing Rottweiler.

Bruiser's role involves posing as a fashion icon rather than performing acrobatics.

In both the original and the sequel, Bruiser was played by Moonie, owned by trainer Sue Chipperton (also owner of Taco Bell's Gidget, who plays Bruiser's mom).

Bruiser's role involves posing as a fashion icon rather than performing acrobatics – he is usually found chilling out in handbags. His best outfits include a red, white and blue jumpsuit; a tutu-like 'skort'; a Jackie O-inspired pink pillbox hat…and some black leather fetish gear to impress Leslie.

 In the bag: Moonie was so fond of Elle's designer handbags that he started jumping into the purses of visitors if they left their bags on the floor.

 Watch the waistline: All the canine clothes had to be refitted each day, depending on how much Moonie had eaten.

Bombón
Bombón El Perro, 2004

Breed: Dogo Argentino

Juan 'Coco' Villegas is down on his luck: he's 52, hasn't seen his wife in 20 years, and loses his job at a petrol station in Patagonia, Argentina. But he's still a kind soul with a sunny outlook. When he stops to help a woman whose car breaks down, she thanks him by gifting him her late father's dog, Bombón. This is not just any ol' fleabag – he's a purebred Dogo Argentino and he has the power to turn Coco's life around.

The award-winning film thrives on the bond between man and his best friend. Dog trainer Walter scouts Bombón as a potential champion show dog and standout stud. Alas, Bombón doesn't seem that keen on the bitches.

Coco thinks he has to give up the dog if he won't bring in any money, but then realizes they belong together. The scene where they are reunited, and Bombón…ahem…gets his groove back, is a moment of pure bliss, evidenced by Coco's ecstatic grin.

Bombón was played by Gregorio, who Argentine director Carlos Sorín described as, 'a very obedient dog'.

The award-winning film thrives on the bond between man and his best friend: the dog is noble, Villegas is humble. It's the perfect pairing in a gem of a film.

 Calm canine: Sorín needed Gregorio to be a restrained actor: 'From when I first read the script I was looking for a dog that was not particularly effusive and affectionate. That would be reserved.'

 No bull: Sorín wrote the script inspired by a bull he once owned, who couldn't be persuaded to mount cows.

Winn-Dixie

Because of Winn-Dixie, 2005

Breed: Berger Picard

It's a classic meet-cute: she's shopping for groceries, he's wreaking havoc knocking boxes over in the produce aisle. That's how Opal, a lonely 10-year-old girl having trouble making friends in her small town in Florida, meets a mutt crashing into the onions. She takes him home and names him after the supermarket, Winn-Dixie.

It's impossible not to fall in love with a smiling dog.

Despite his shaggy look, Winn-Dixie isn't a mutt at all. The film is adapted from the beloved children's novel of the same name, and director Wayne Wang wanted to appease readers by bringing to life the shaggy illustrated dog on its cover. So he chose dogs of the rare French breed Berger Picard to play Winn-Dixie.

There were a total of five French dogs imported for the shoot; the bulk of the role was split between two dogs with different personalities; trainer Mark Forbes said Lyco was 'one of the goofiest dogs I've ever trained', while Scott was 'good at more intimate scenes'.

It's an impressive canine performance, both in facial expressions (and ear twitches) and in action sequences on the baseball field and in the paddling pool. Those grins aren't CGI movie wizardry; this breed can appear to smile in real life. Who can resist a smiling dog?

For the birds: In the pet store, Gertrude the parrot doesn't actually land on the dog's head – the bird perched on a fake furry dog head against a green screen, and the filmmakers then added the dog in post-production.

Treat time: Actress AnnaSophia Robb, aged nine when the film shot, tasted the liver treats that she gave the dogs throughout shooting. Her verdict? 'They are pretty good.'

Maya

Eight Below, 2006

Breed: Alaskan Malamute

This moving story – loosely inspired by the 1958 Japanese expedition that also inspired the 1998 Japanese film *Antarctica* – is about the survival skills of a pack of dogs stranded in Antarctica; and the dedication of one man (Jerry, played by Paul Walker) to try to save the dogs he left behind.

The dogs all have distinct personalities on screen.

There are eight main dogs in the pack, a mix of Siberian huskies, Alaskan malamutes and Greenland dogs, all with distinct personalities: Maya, played by seven-year-olds Koda Bear and Jasmine; Max, played by D.J. and Timba; Old Jack, played by Apache and Buck; Shadow, played by Noble and Troika; Buck, played by Flapjack and Dino; Truman, played by Sitka and Chase; Dewey, played by Floyd and Ryan; and Shorty, played by Jasper and Lightning.

Head trainer Mike Alexander of Birds & Animals said, 'We were looking for dogs with unique looks, great personalities and a love of learning.' In all, 30 dogs were used.

Director Frank Marshall said of Koda Bear, 'it was like he had read the script. He acted like he was in charge.'

Sadly, not all of the pack survives their six-month ordeal, which makes Maya's reunion with Jerry all the more poignant.

Sealed deal: The scary scene with the seal was shot with a fake seal smeared with baby food and peanut butter, and meaty bones hidden inside.

Royal treatment: Koda Bear was known as 'The Princess' because she would not go anywhere without her special blanket. She also starred in *Snow Dogs* and TV's *Malcolm In the Middle*.

Shaggy
The Shaggy Dog, 2006

Breed: Bearded Collie

The advertising slogan 'Be More Dog' would be a good tagline for *The Shaggy Dog*. Tim Allen stars as Dave, a district attorney who morphs into a bearded collie named Shaggy (thanks to some magic DNA from a 300-year-old Tibetan dog named Khyi Yang Po). Workaholic Dave gains a new perspective on life, and becomes a better human being (even starting to rally against animal testing).

A total of seven bearded collies played Shaggy, with a dog named Cole performing most of the action (he was trained by veteran Mark Forbes). In addition to a lot of barking on command, he does a number of specific tricks like leaping off furniture, digging in a backpack, catching Frisbees and running over cars. There was of course some CGI wizardry, like when Shaggy and his animal friends are meditating.

'Cole was amazing. It was literally freaky how good that dog was.'

Cole looks marvellous on screen – a furry coat that flows in the wind, an expressive face and bulbous black nose, and a long tongue that flops out hilariously.

Allen said, 'Cole was amazing. They had an animatronic dog that we didn't even use. It was literally freaky how good that dog was.'

Sniffing around: In the scene where a German shepherd has to sniff out Tim Allen's backside in an elevator, they put a meat smell on the inside of Allen's thighs. 'The dog didn't leave my crotch alone', he said.

Pane and gain: In the scene where Shaggy runs into a store window, the dog's face was filmed with a glass pane – which crew members moved upwards – on a green screen.

Sam

I Am Legend, 2007

Breed: German Shepherd

Scientist Robert Neville (played by Will Smith) thinks he's the last man on Earth after a virus has wiped out humanity. But he's not alone; he's got Sam (short for Samantha), a gift from his late daughter.

They eat dinner together (like any good kid, Sam doesn't eat enough of her veggies), they joyride around town together in a Mustang Shelby, they hit the treadmill together, they huddle in the bathtub to avoid the infected creatures. Neville talks to Sam and serenades her with Bob Marley songs. He becomes an even more broken man when he has to say goodbye to Sam (you might want to prepare yourself by logging onto doesthedogdie.com).

While many of the creatures are computer-generated, Sam was wonderfully real. She was mostly played by a three-year-old German shepherd named Abbey, who was rescued from a kennel and trained quickly for the shoot. There were also two back-up dogs, Kona and Sammy.

Mirroring the bond between Neville and Sam, Will Smith and Abbey 'really developed their own bond,' said trainer Steve **Will Smith understood that this was his co-star.** Berens. 'He understood that this was his co-star, and he really got into it. I think that she really liked him, and that made a difference.'

 Dating game: Before production in New York, Will Smith went on 'dates' in Los Angeles with Abbey to get to know her better.

 Adoption bid: Will Smith became so fond of Abbey, that he tried (unsuccessfully) to adopt her from the trainer.

Papi
Beverly Hills Chihuahua, 2008

Breed: Chihuahua

There are many great canine performances in *Beverly Hills Chihuahua*, including one by petite Angel, the white deer head Chihuahua, as Chloe, but Papi actor Rusco, a Chihuahua mix, has attitude to spare.

Trainer Mike Alexander was looking for a new canine actor and found Rusco's profile posted online by a Southern California dog shelter. He was drawn in by his big ears and expressive face. Alexander said, 'When we got to meet him at the shelter, he had a great bouncy personality.' After six months of training, Rusco was ready for his close-up.

Papi belongs to a landscaper working at a Beverly Hills mansion where pampered Chloe swans around in her Chanel outfits and Harry Winston collar. When Chloe goes to Mexico and is dognapped, Papi helps rescue his '*mi corazón*' and she finally realizes she's loved him all along.

'He's a romantic dog, but he's got a little bit of street in him.'

The production showcases 200 dogs (handled by 60 animal trainers), with digital effects used later to help them 'talk'. The only fully computer-generated animals in the film were the rat and iguana.

Actor George Lopez, a Chihuahua owner himself and the voice of Papi, thought Rusco was perfectly cast. 'He's a romantic dog, but he's got a little bit of street in him.'

 Baby face: When Chloe is near death and Papi has to lick her, baby food was put on Angel's face to encourage Rusco.

 Bilingual barkers: On set, some of the dogs understood English, while others only recognized commands in Spanish.

Lucy
Wendy & Lucy, 2008

Breed: Mixed Breed

In this minimalist but powerful drama, Michelle Williams stars as a vulnerable young woman living off the grid in contemporary America. She's broke and sleeping in her car in Oregon when her beloved mutt Lucy goes missing.

Remarkably, director Kelly Reichardt cast her own rescue dog Lucy, who had already played a smaller role in her earlier film *Old Joy*.

Reichardt said, 'She was never trained…I just let her be herself. It's a good way to keep an actor in the moment – they are responding to a dog and you don't know what the dog will do.'

Williams had a natural rapport with Lucy that comes across on screen. Lucy, aged six when the film was shot, isn't required **Lucy is wonderful as woman's best friend.** to do any special tricks, but she's wonderful as woman's best friend – she knows when to trot along by Wendy's side, when to fetch a stick, and just when to give the right whimper, bark, head tilt or doleful look.

The description on the lost-pup posters say it all: 'floppy ears, sharp eyes, yellowish brown, friendly face'. Williams delivers a quietly poignant performance – when she gets a call that Lucy is okay, the smile that emerges on her face is priceless.

 Stick to it: Sometimes the film crew would put a stick in Williams' backpack so Lucy would follow her.

 Editing room: Reichardt jokes that Lucy 'didn't seem to understand the editing process at all.' The filmmaker cut the film in her apartment and anytime she'd work on the dog pound scene, Lucy would 'bark her head off' when she heard the sounds of the other dogs.

Marley

Marley & Me, 2008

Breed: Labrador Retriever

In this crowd-pleasing hit, adapted from the bestselling memoir of the same name, newspaper columnist John Grogan (Owen Wilson) and his wife Jenny (Jennifer Aniston) adopt a hapless Labrador retriever, soon dubbed 'the world's worst dog'. Naughty Marley quickly becomes an essential part of the growing Grogan family, despite knocking the head off a snowman, humping the leg of his obedience trainer (the formidable Kathleen Turner), and gnawing on everything from precious jewellery to the sofa.

'I wanted to work him to let him be even crazier than he already was.'

The film employed 22 dogs (including 11 puppies) to play Marley during his 13-year life. The main Marley was a three-year-old named Clyde, while 14-year-old Copper played him in old age.

Trainer Mathilde de Cagny lovingly remembers overzealous Clyde as 'out of this world crazy. He was loving and a big, big dog full of energy and absolutely cuckoo…I wanted to work him to let him be even crazier than he already was.' This included encouraging him to tear up old furniture to prepare for the role.

De Cagny said, 'Jennifer and Owen got surprised many times with what Clyde did. We wanted the dog to be a dog.' Occasionally director David Frankel filmed the dogs during rehearsals – sometimes their unpredictable behaviour would result in the best 'take'.

 On the ball: Owen Wilson's own Australian cattle dog, Garcia, has a small cameo in the baseball park scene.

 Writer's room: The book's author, John Grogan, appears as the cocker spaniel owner in the dog training class.

Hachi

Hachi: A Dog's Tale, 2009

Breed: Akita

In this simple but moving story about a dog's loyalty, the titular dog is a devoted Akita who loves his owner (played by Richard Gere) so much that he waits at the train station for him for 10 years after his death. It's not just a Greyfriars Bobby rip-off: the fact that it is inspired by a true Japanese story of a dog born in 1923 makes it all the more poignant.

Richard Gere gamely crawls around with a tennis ball in his mouth.

The film boasts a great pedigree, both canine and human: Oscar-winning director Lasse Hallström, an A-list cast led by Richard Gere and Joan Allen, and three regal Akitas (two-year-old siblings Layla and Chico plus four-year-old Forrest) were used by trainer Mark Harden to play Hachi. To play Hachi as a puppy, they cast a smaller Shiba Inu (another ancient Japanese breed).

Gere, a dog lover working on this passion project, gamely crawls around with a tennis ball in his mouth, trying to teach Hachi to fetch. As, the actor explained Akitas aren't easily bribed by food like other dogs, and it took him three days on set to earn their trust.

The Akitas, who are known for their independent nature and strong will, were also a challenge for Harden. Chico barely looked at him for a month, so instead of teaching him commands like sit, stay and speak, he taught him tasks on an agility course.

 Help the aged: The elderly, frail Hachi at the end of the film was actually played by four-year-old Forrest. He acts with an impressive limp and was trained to move cautiously on dozens of small marks. He looks older thanks to fur makeup and groomer's chalk. Tiny weighted magnets were used to make his ears and tail droop.

 Coming to America: After visiting Japan, Helen Keller brought the first Akita to America in 1937.

Romeo
Hotel For Dogs, 2009

Breed: Chinese Crested

In a film full of delightful dogs, little Romeo is a standout, partly because Chinese cresteds are more commonly seen in 'ugliest dog' contests.

Romeo is left unwanted at a pet store when he joins a group of scrappy strays at the Hotel For Dogs, a pooch paradise created by four kids to save their furry friends from the shelter. Romeo hangs with terriers Friday and Georgia, mastiff Lenny, English bulldog Cooper, Beauceron Henry, and border collie Shep; but of course he mostly has eyes for his Juliet, a perfect white poodle he woos with a kiss and a romantic interlude on the roof.

Chinese cresteds are more commonly seen in 'ugliest dog' contests.

Thanks to gender-blind casting, Dolly, a female Chinese crested, was the main actor for Romeo (she could lift her leg higher than the male dogs), and Dash, a male poodle, played Juliet.

In the hotel, the dogs enjoy ingenious inventions like a road trip simulator, a fetch machine, a poop room, a bespoke fire hydrant toilet and a vending machine for old shoes to chew on.

The production employed nearly 70 dogs – including *Beginners'* Cosmo as Friday. The filmmakers had an important message at the end of the credits: 'Help shelter dogs find loving homes.'

 Kiss and tell: To get Romeo and Juliet to kiss in two scenes, a thin piece of plastic covered with baby food was held between them, and the dogs licked it, making it look like they were kissing.

 A breed apart: Other Chinese crested dogs in films include Peek in *Cats & Dogs*, Fluffy in *102 Dalmations*, Giuseppe in *Marmaduke*, and Krull from *How to Lose a Guy in 10 Days*.

Arthur
Beginners, 2010

Breed: Jack Russell Terrier

In this playful and poignant drama, Arthur isn't a prop or a show dog performing tricks, he's a real member of the family. Arthur first belongs to Hal (Christopher Plummer). His son Oliver (Ewan McGregor) adopts the dog after Hal is diagnosed with terminal cancer. Oliver is coming to terms with losing his father, as well as his dad's later-life coming out (based on the director's own experience), and at the same time falling in love with a French actress (Mélanie Laurent). Arthur is beside him during the ups and downs, and even has some insightful – subtitled – conversations with his master.

McGregor also fell in love with the canine actor, Cosmo. The dog became so comfortable on the set that you can spot him napping in the Halloween party scene.

Trainer Mathilde de Cagny rescued Cosmo when he was about two and a half years old, and described him as an energetic pup who can 'turn on and be total terrier, but he can really be mellow and gentle'.

Cosmo became so comfortable on the set that you can spot him napping during the Halloween party scene.

Cosmo was so relaxed acting with McGregor that de Cagny wasn't even in the room for some scenes. De Cagny added, 'Ewan and Cosmo connected in real ways that could never be acted.'

 To dye for: Vegetable dye was used to make Cosmo look more like Bowser, the 13-year-old terrier who director Mike Mills inherited from his father in real life.

 Early adopter: Ewan McGregor was so attached to Cosmo that he adopted a dog of his own, a poodle mix called Sid, on the last day of the shoot. They later occasionally reunited with de Cagny and Cosmo for walks.

Marmaduke

Marmaduke, 2010

Breed: Great Dane

The trouble with dog movies using obvious CGI moments like dogs dancing and surfing is that you start to wonder if the canines only exist in a computer. That's not the case with the first live-action film of *Marmaduke*, inspired by the long-running comic strip. Two-thirds of the movie features real canine actors…80 of them.

The gangly Great Dane and his family move from Kansas to California; he helps to bring them together as well as breaking through the canine cliques at the dog park.

The animals interact with people but also exist in a sort of parallel universe where they can hear each other talk and host their own game nights and fabulous parties.

Great Danes, with their bumbling huge bodies and drooling faces, are made for the big screen.

Great Danes, with their bumbling huge bodies and drooling faces, are made for the big screen, especially in terms of physical comedy.

George and his half brother Spirit (weighing in at 160-plus pounds each) were the two ginormous Great Danes who played Marmaduke (voiced by Owen Wilson). As director Tom Dey explained, 'George was the dog we needed to hit his marks, and Spirit was the one we needed to break down walls.'

 Fresh meat: Head trainer Michael Alexander invented 'meat glasses' – sunglasses rigged with a dog treat so the dog would maintain the correct eyeline when looking at the human actors.

 Prick up your ears: For scenes when Marmaduke's ears perk up, a monofilament line was attached so a crew member could gently pull them up.

The Dog

The Artist, 2011

Breed: Parson Russell Terrier

The wildly talented Uggie delivers one of the best canine film roles in many decades in this Oscar-winning film, which is a twinkling tribute to the golden age of Hollywood.

The Dog serves as the companion to silent film star George Valentin (the role that won Jean Dujardin an Oscar), who performs with George as well as being his talented sidekick off screen. The Dog can walk on his hind legs, play dead, bury his head in his paws, jump into George's arms, and even mirror George's movements (especially funny at the dining table as George eats his breakfast).

In a scene straight out of Lassie's playbook, the Dog also saves George from a fire, running to fetch a cop.

Uggie will always be remembered for his magnificent skill with physical comedy.

Californian canine Uggie become suitably famous himself, walking many a red carpet and hamming it up on an international press tour for *The Artist.*

Trainer Omar von Muller saved Uggie from going to the pound, and soon realized how smart and hard-working he was.

Uggie will always be remembered for his magnificent skill with physical comedy; director Michel Hazanavicius didn't have most of the dog's tricks in the original script, only adding in these scene-stealing moments when he met Uggie and saw his captivating moves.

 Sneaky sausages: In the fire scene, on-set trainer Sarah Clifford hid small bits of hot dog around Jean Dujardin, so although Uggie is seen loyally rushing to his master, he is really sniffing for food.

 Oscar glory: Uggie made a surprise cameo appearance on the 2012 Oscar telecast; there had been a passionate but unsuccessful campaign to allow him to be nominated for Best Supporting Actor.

Red Dog

Red Dog, 2011

Breed: Kelpie

Red Dog was inspired by a real dog who charmed everyone in the Pilbara region of Western Australia in the 1970s, becoming a local legend.

Red Dog is a stray who makes friends easily – especially among the town's macho iron miners – and becomes especially attached to an American bus driver, John Grant (Josh Lucas).

Red Dog hitchhikes and shares his spectacular flatulence; he interrupts a date at the drive-in; he jumps on the back of John's motorcycle; he holds the yarn for a local knitter; he fights with Red Cat; he even saves a man from a shark attack. And when he can't find his master, he searches across Australia for him.

Red Dog is a stray who makes friends easily.

A kelpie named Koko, who started life as a show dog, delivers a marvellous performance after being cast for his particularly expressive face. Producer Nelson Woss referred to him as a particularly 'chilled-out kelpie'.

Animal trainer Luke Hura taught Koko more than 60 commands for the role (including snarling, crawling and looking straight at the camera). Hura said that Koko 'learnt how to communicate…That's the type of dog Red Dog was. He really started to work things out with humans.'

 Hot seat: Koko took five weeks of training for a scene in which he learns to push an actress off her bus seat. First he pushed a bag off, then a dummy, then a person.

 Dedicated director: *Red Dog* director Kriv Stenders is allergic to dogs, so he couldn't touch Koko (and he took a lot of antihistamines during the shoot).

Banjo

Sightseers, 2012

Breed: Parson Russell Terrier

This pitch-perfect black comedy is exquisite in its details: knitted crotchless knickers, a giant souvenir from the Keswick Pencil Museum, and an innocent white terrier who offsets the depraved behaviour of the humans.

Alice Lowe and Steve Oram wrote the hilarious screenplay and star as Tina and Chris, two misfit lovers on a caravan holiday in England, evolving as serial killers along the way (think *Nuts in May* meets *Bonnie and Clyde*). They dognap a Parson Russell terrier named Banjo, who Tina suspects is the reincarnation of her mum's departed doggo Poppy. The pup's poo emerges as a plot point inspiring another killing.

Banjo is that rare beast – a calm terrier – with a quizzical look on his face and a perfect tilt of the head.

Banjo is that rare beast – a calm terrier – with a quizzical look on his face and a perfect tilt of the head. Two-year-old Smurf played Banjo, and in a short flashback scene, Ged played Poppy.

Smurf, also a veteran of TV and commercials, was a quick learner, 'confidently working to hand signals from a distance', said his owner Sarah Humphreys. He learned to skateboard, limp, nail a handstand, put a teabag in a mug and simulate urinating. After all that, going camping with a couple of serial killers was a breeze.

 If the caravan's rocking: Smurf won the Palm Dog Award at the 2012 Cannes Film Festival. Awards founder Toby Rose praised the film's hilarious sex scene: 'The dog gatecrashes some lovemaking in a way that elicits screams of shock from the audience.'

 How's tricks: In 2017, Smurf earned a spot in the Guinness World Records for most tricks performed by a dog in one minute (32!).

Bonny
Seven Psychopaths, 2012

Breed: Shih Tzu

Bonny is definitely the sweet centre of this black comedy caper.

Billy (Sam Rockwell) and Hans (Christopher Walken) play crooks who dognap pups for the ransom money. They pick the wrong target when they grab Bonny, the beloved bow-wow of violent gangster Charlie (Woody Harrelson). Colin Farrell plays Marty, Billy's friend, who is an alcoholic screenwriter trying to write a movie about seven psychopaths and comes in contact with a few real ones.

All the guys in the film – even the ones who turn out to be psychopaths – dote on this fuzzy little lass.

Bonny exudes serenity throughout the film.

Director McDonagh cast Bonny, an eight-pound, one-year-old imperial shih tzu adopted by the Performing Animal Troupe. Bonny formerly lived in a mobile home in East Los Angeles, had absolutely no training, and wasn't even good at socializing.

Trainer Claire Dore brought Bonny out of her shell, but she said the dog retained a 'calm quietness bordering on apathy' – perfect for the role.

Bonny exudes serenity throughout the film, whether snoozing on Colin Farrell's head, sitting by the campfire in Joshua Tree, or lounging around ignoring an epic shootout.

Name game: The dog's name in the script had always been Bonny, and the role went to a real dog who was remarkably already named Bonny (short for Bonita). It was meant to be.

Feel the noise: In shootout scenes, Bonny's welfare was always in mind, and the filmmakers carefully adhered to safe noise guidelines for animals. If it was ever too much for Bonny, a stuffed toy double was used instead.

Hagen
White God, 2014

Breed: Mixed Breed

More than 250 dogs were used in the production of Hungarian film *White God*, canine cinema's highest achievement. This potent political parable tells the story of a young girl, Lili, whose father doesn't allow her to keep her beloved dog Hagen because of Budapest's 'mutt tax'. When Hagen is sent to an overcrowded shelter, he leads hundreds of dogs to rise up against their human oppressors.

Seeing 200 real dogs taking over the city is a stunning sight, as is the (spooky) final scene, with packs of dogs lying down in front of Lili in eerie stillness.

> **Hagen leads hundreds of dogs to rise up against their human oppressors.**

Hired to play the leader of the pack, Hagen, were Arizona-born brothers Bodie and Luke – likely a Labrador/shar-pei mix. They were discovered and trained by Teresa Ann Miller in Los Angeles, and then went to Hungary to shoot the film when they were 13 months old.

The voluminous packs of dogs in Hungary were trained by Arpad Halasz, using mostly dogs from local rescue centres. During pre-production, the two trainers would check in with each other on video calls to monitor their dogs' progress.

The acting rescue dogs had a happy ending. After the shooting ended, almost all were adopted and found new homes.

 Floored: In the scene where Hagen is given a tranquillizer and the director wanted a reaction from the dog, Miller sprayed a shiny coat treatment on Luke's fur, which made him rub himself on the floor.

 Nailed it: In the dogfighting scenes, trainers put rubber caps on the dogs' claws so they wouldn't accidentally scratch each other. Luke saw it as a fun 'play date'.

Rocco
The Drop, 2014

Breed: Pit Bull

In *The Drop*, Tom Hardy rescues a puppy. There may be some other distracting plot going on – a robbery at a bar gone wrong, menacing gangsters, etc. But really: Tom. Puppy. That's all you need to remember.

Hardy plays Brooklyn bartender Bob, who finds an abused puppy in a rubbish bin and rescues it with the help of another loner, Nadia (Noomi Rapace). He thinks it's a boxer, but it's actually a pit bull, who he names Rocco. The breed gets a boost from the script – Bob initially thinks pit bulls are dangerous dogs, but as Nadia says, this puppy is 'nothing but sweet'.

Director Michaël R. Roskam didn't want Rocco doing any fancy tricks – 'I just wanted it to be a dog', he said. Bob – who has shut himself off emotionally for a **Pit bulls are a breed that is so traditionally misunderstood.** decade – softens every time he's around the lovable pup. The casting of a pit bull was intentional – as Roskam explained, 'it's a breed that is so traditionally misunderstood'. Just like Bob.

Three slate-grey pit bull puppies played Rocco, starting with the 11-week- old T. Trainer Kim Krafsky explained, 'We just tried to make everything a game.'

 Sleepover: The animal trainer often 'lent' Tom Hardy a dog for the night when he was lonely during the shoot in New York.

 Dogman: Tom Hardy is a huge dog aficionado and has a pit bull tattoo on his back. He has said, 'I love dogs and I see myself as a dog inside in many ways.'

Max

Max, 2015

Breed: Belgian Malinois

Dogs can get PTSD, too. That's what happens to Max, a military service dog traumatized by the death of his handler Kyle in Afghanistan. The dog is so distressed that the Marines threaten to put him down, until Kyle's family back in Texas – especially younger brother Justin – help to heal the dog while also healing their grief too.

Animal coordinator Mark Forbes employed six Malinois as Max. The handsome three-year-old Carlos – sleek and noble with particularly impressive pointed ears – was the lead dog and used for 80 per cent of the role.

Forbes found Carlos on a Kentucky farm after a nationwide search. He was camera ready with his uniquely light facial markings (which show more emotion on screen) and focused personality. The dog was more temperamental than most canine actors, but delivered well on the set after extensive training.

Carlos is sleek and noble with particularly impressive pointed ears.

Rescue dog Jagger (who went on to star in TV's *Angie Tribeca*), Pax (the fastest runner), Dude (the best jumper), Pilot and Chaos were used as Carlos's doubles.

Max is a character of great range – from silently curling up on the floor in front of Kyle's casket at the funeral, to scaling tall fences and tackling bad guys and their Rottweilers to foil a shady arms deal.

 On the job: Josh Wiggins, the actor who played Justin, went on the job with his dad, who works with bomb-sniffing dogs for the Houston Police Department, to get more comfortable with working dogs.

 Dye job: Once Carlos was selected as the main actor for Max, the five other Malinois had their faces professionally died to match Carlos's unique facial markings.

Wiener-Dog
Wiener-Dog, 2016

Breed: Dachshund

Misanthrope Todd Solondz directs this portmanteau of four stories about flawed humans, each connected by one dachshund. A suburban father adopts the dog for his son Remi, who is recovering from cancer. From there, Wiener-Dog (as Remi calls him) gets sick and is taken to be put down, where he's saved by a vet technician named Dawn. She renames him Doody and takes him on a road trip, before he's passed to a frustrated screenwriting teacher, and finally to a bitter elderly woman (who renames him Cancer).

The dachshund is handsome and dignified, even when the humans aren't. Thankfully, the dachshund is handsome and dignified, even when the humans aren't – whether he's riding a skateboard; sitting on Danny DeVito's lap on a New York bus; or curled up on the sofa with Ellen Burstyn. Still, most dog lovers might want to stop watching before the disturbing finale.

Five dogs played the role: Little Hope, Big Hope, Vodka, Ruby and Rozie. 'The one thing they all had in common was their stupidity', cranky director Solondz said. But dachshund admirers can ignore that sentiment and thrill to the film's idiosyncratic intermission: the dachshund walks mountains, prairies and other iconic backdrops to an extremely catchy ditty called 'The Ballad of Wiener-Dog'.

 Walking the dog: For the intermission, the dog was filmed on a treadmill. Solondz said, 'We had the whole crew standing around while the dog tried to walk on the treadmill, and after three hours we did get 12 seconds of usable footage.'

 Beast of burden: Solondz said the film was inspired by Robert Bresson's 1966 film *Au Hasard Balthazar*, about a donkey passed from owner to owner.

Bailey

A Dog's Purpose, 2017

Breed: Red Retriever

What is the meaning of life? This opening line of *A Dog's Purpose* signals that this isn't a ditzy dog flick. The film grapples with big existential questions as one dog's soul moves across five decades and is reincarnated in different breeds, with an interior monologue voiced by Josh Gad.

We first meet mutt Toby, who becomes retriever Bailey, then German shepherd Ellie, then corgi Tino, then Australian shepherd/Saint Bernard mix Buddy.

Director Lasse Hallström encouraged improvisation for the dogs.

Bailey gets the most screen time; trainer Mark Forbes thought red retriever Trip had 'both the temperament to be trained and a special look that showed some great character'. Bailey's best tricks are chasing his own tail in spectacular style, and jumping over his young master Ethan's back to catch an old football.

Director Lasse Hallström encouraged improvisation: 'Trip did things that were unexpected...but, like a good actor, his choices worked.'

It's impossible to have a dry eye when an older Ethan meets the lumbering Buddy and realizes he might be his old companion Bailey, back to chase footballs again decades later. And what does this omniscient dog discover to be its ultimate purpose? To 'be here now.'

 Cross breeds: In all, 29 puppies and dogs played the five leads; 70 canine extras were also recruited.

 For the dogs: Dog lover Lasse Hallström directed two other canine-centric films: *My Life as a Dog* and *Hachi: A Dog's Tale.*

Patrick

Patrick, 2018

Breed: Pug

It's any dog owner's nightmare: stepping barefoot in wet dog food. That's just one of the puggy problems caused by Patrick.

Sarah is living a chaotic single life in London when her situation changes overnight: she gets a new job as an English teacher, and her grandmother bequeaths her a spoiled pug named Patrick. Sarah doesn't think she's a dog person, but perhaps Patrick can change her mind.

Patrick was played by Harley, a formerly shy pug trained by Julie Tottman to perform unique moves like stepping on a pedal bin, taking packets of meat from a fridge, jumping up and down on a sofa, dashing across a bridge and riding on boats.

Patrick also sports some impressive outfits like a chic trenchcoat or a dapper tuxedo.

Patrick's little smushy pug face, with brilliantly bulbous eyes, is hard to resist. He also sports some impressive outfits: a chic trenchcoat for walks in the park, and a dapper tuxedo for granny's funeral.

Harley relished the filming experience. According to director Mandie Fletcher, 'On his days off he used to stand outside [trainer] Julie's bedroom door because he wanted to go to work. So he enjoyed himself.'

 A meaty role: The dog was so professional that human star Beattie Edmondson said it took some coaxing for him to lick her face – some pâté was used as encouragement (not fun when the dog licked some of it into the vegetarian actress's mouth).

 Family affair: The real Patrick, a black pug belonging to screenwriter Vanessa Davies, appears in the end credits.

Acknowledgements

This book is dedicated to Scotty, My Good Boy

Special thanks to Scott Murray, Neal and Brenda Mitchell, Margaret Murray and the brilliant team at Laurence King: in particular Donald Dinwiddie, Sara Goldsmith and John Parton.

Thanks to American Humane, BFI Reuben Library, Mathilde de Cagny, Claire Dore, Hadley Freeman, Sarah Humphreys, imdb, Alice Lowe, Alan McArthur, Teresa Ann Miller, Kelly Reichardt, Toby Rose, Julie Tottman and Nelson Woss.

A special woof for Snickers (RIP), Seamus, Siegfried, Hamish, Ginger and Arthur.

—Wendy Mitchell

Credits

Front cover *Uggie*, 2012. ©nickholt.com; **Back cover** *A Dog's Life*, 1918. First National/Kobal/Rex/Shutterstock; **6–7** Entertainment Pictures/Alamy; **8** First National/Kobal/REX/Shutterstock; **10** Kobal/REX/Shutterstock; **12** Archive PL/Alamy; **14** Snap/REX/Shutterstock; **17** Entertainment Pictures/Alamy; **19** MGM/Kobal/REX/Shutterstock; **20** Everett Collection Inc./Alamy; **22** TCD/Prod.DB/Alamy; **25** Disney/Kobal/REX/Shutterstock; **26 top** Moviestore/REX/Shutterstock; **26 bottom** Disney/Kobal/REX/Shutterstock; **28** United Archives GmbH/Alamy; **31** 20th Century Fox/Kobal/REX/Shutterstock; **33** Cinerama/Kobal/REX/Shutterstock; **35** Everett Collection Inc./Alamy; **37** Mulberry Square/Kobal/REX/Shutterstock; **39** Moviestore Collection Ltd/Alamy; **41 top** AF Archive/Alamy; **41 bottom** Paramount/Kobal/REX/Shutterstock; **42** Sportsphoto/Alamy; **45** Photo 12/Alamy; **46** Moviestore Collection Ltd/Alamy; **48 top** Moviestore/REX/Shutterstock; **48 bottom** Universal/Kobal/REX/Shutterstock; **50** Disney/Kobal/REX/Shutterstock; **53** PictureLux/The Hollywood Archive/Alamy; **55** Moviestore/REX/Shutterstock; **56** 20th Century Fox/Kobal/REX/Shutterstock; **59** AF Archive/Alamy; **60 top** Everett Collection Inc./Alamy; **60 bottom** Entertainment Pictures/Alamy; **62** Kharen Hill/Walt Disney/Kobal/REX/Shutterstock; **65 top** Moviestore/REX/Shutterstock; **65 bottom** Alex Bailey/Rysher/Kobal/REX/Shutterstock; **66** Tristar/Gracie/Kobal/REX/Shutterstock; **69** AF Archive/Alamy; **70** Warner Bros/Kobal/REX/Shutterstock; **73** Doane Gregory/Castle Rock/Warner Bros/Kobal/REX/Shutterstock; **74 top** Myles Aronowitz/Avery Pix/New Line/Kobal/REX/Shutterstock; **74 bottom** Photo 12/Alamy; **76** Warner Bros/Kobal/REX/Shutterstock; **79** Moviestore/REX/Shutterstock; **80** Melinda Sue Gordon/Columbia/Kobal/REX/Shutterstock; **83** Sam Emerson/Mgm/Kobal/REX/Shutterstock; **85 top** TCD/Prod.DB/Alamy; **85 bottom** Guacamole/Ok/Kobal/REX/Shutterstock; **86** Everett Collection Inc./Alamy; **88** Moviestore/REX/Shutterstock; **91 top** AF Archive/Alamy; **91 bottom** Disney/Kobal/REX/Shutterstock; **92 top** Everett Collection Inc./Alamy; **92 centre** TCD/Prod.DB/Alamy; **92 bottom** Barry Wetcher/Warner Bros/Kobal/REX/Shutterstock; **95** Disney/Kobal/REX/Shutterstock; **96** Field Guide/Film Science/Glass Eye/Kobal/REX/Shutterstock; **99 top** Moviestore/REX/Shutterstock; **99 bottom** Kobal/REX/Shutterstock; **100** AF Archive/Alamy; **103 top** Everett Collection Inc./Alamy; **103 bottom** Moviestore/REX/Shutterstock; **104** Olympus Pictures/Kobal/REX/Shutterstock; **106** Twentieth Century Fox Film Corporation/Kobal/REX/Shutterstock; **108** La Classe Americaine/Ufilm/Kobal/REX/Shutterstock; **110 top** Woss Group/Kobal/REX/Shutterstock; **110 bottom** AF Archive/Alamy; **112** TCD/Prod.DB/Alamy; **114** Blueprint Pictures/Kobal/REX/Shutterstock; **117** Proton Cinema/Pola Pandora Filmproduktions/Chimney Pot/Film I Vast/Hnff/Zdf/Arte/Kobal/REX/Shutterstock; **118 top** AF Archive/Alamy; **118 bottom** Barry Wetcher/Chernin/Fox Serchlight/Kobal/REX/Shutterstock; **120** Jeffrey Mayer/Pictorial Press Ltd/Alamy; **123** REX/Shutterstock; **125** Suzanne Hanover/Universal/Kobal/REX/Shutterstock; **127** AF Archive/Alamy

Acknowledgements

This book is dedicated to Scotty, My Good Boy

Special thanks to Scott Murray, Neal and Brenda Mitchell, Margaret Murray and the brilliant team at Laurence King: in particular Donald Dinwiddie, Sara Goldsmith and John Parton.

Thanks to American Humane, BFI Reuben Library, Mathilde de Cagny, Claire Dore, Hadley Freeman, Sarah Humphreys, imdb, Alice Lowe, Alan McArthur, Teresa Ann Miller, Kelly Reichardt, Toby Rose, Julie Tottman and Nelson Woss.

A special woof for Snickers (RIP), Seamus, Siegfried, Hamish, Ginger and Arthur.

—Wendy Mitchell

Credits